VIA DOLOROSA

THE STATIONS OF THE CROSS

Lenten Meditations

by

Diane Zike

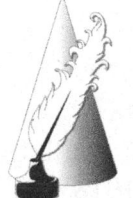

Foolscap & Quill

Back cover image courtesy of Istockphoto.com
11582105

Front cover by Foolscap & Quill, LLC

ISBN 978-1-938143-00-7

ISBN 978-1-938143-20-5

UPC 803236700109

Published by:
Foolscap & Quill, LLC
P. O. Box 1018
Morrison, CO 80465-1018
www.foolscap-quill.com

Dedicated to my Lord and Savior Jesus Christ

in humble gratitude

for the salvation of my soul

Introduction

The *Via Dolorosa*

Via Dolorosa (Lat. "sorrowful way") or Via Crucis (Lat. "the way of the Cross") is the path believed to be taken by Jesus from the place of his condemnation by Pilate to Mount Golgotha, the site of his crucifixion, and then to his grave site. Early Christians continued the ancient Jewish practice of pilgrimages to Jerusalem. Out of this practice came the tradition of the Stations of the Cross as a series of commemorative devotions or meditations.

Following the Stations of the Cross requires us to focus on the passion and death of our Lord Jesus Christ. That is not easy. So much pain and suffering, so much grief is hard to bear. It has been said to me that the Stations of the Cross are too painful; recalling the suffering of Jesus is too much. How can it be too much for us when it was not too much for our Lord and Savior to take up that cross and to die for us?

I attended a screening of the *Passion of Christ*, a movie by Mel Gibson, that presented a very graphic portrayal of the suffering of Jesus. During one of the horrible scenes of Jesus being beaten a woman got up and hurried out of theater announcing that she "could not bear it any more." What about the people who were there? What about Jesus' mother and others who knew him as brother, neighbor, friend? How did they bear it? How best for us to know something of that passion and pain?

I am not a fan of graphic violence in movies or on television; there is more than enough real violence in the world. Sometimes I, too, turn away. At the same time I believe we must face the passion of our Lord boldly; we must embrace it. It is in Jesus' passion and death that we find life, our life. When we walk with Jesus on the *Via Dolorosa* we join in his suffering and in his death. By that act of mutual suffering, by embracing our Lord's death, we also embrace the eternal life that his death offers to us.

Although we can never be ready to bear pain and suffering, the time has come to begin that final journey with Jesus. The Via Dolorosa awaits us. Let us begin. Take up your cross and follow Jesus.

*Assist us mercifully with your help, O Lord God of our salvation, that we may enter with joy upon the contemplation of those mighty acts, whereby you have given us life and immortality; through Jesus Christ our Lord. Amen. (*Palm Sunday liturgy, *Book of Common Prayer,* 270)

Ash Wednesday

Early in the Ash Wednesday Service we are invited to an observance of a Holy Lent with these words: "Dear People of God: The First Christians observed with great devotion the days of our Lord's passion and resurrection." (Ash Wednesday Liturgy, *Book of Common Prayer,* 264) Those early observances became ritualized in the Stations of the Cross that we meditate on here.

We begin our first steps in Lent and on the Via Dolorosa with the reminder that the journey is from passion and death to resurrection joy. The journey through Lent and following the Stations is a difficult one. There is much to remember, to reflect upon, to repent, but if we are steadfast in our journey following Jesus, salvation awaits us.

What must we do during this holy season, during this commemoration of our Lord's passion and death? We must examine our conscience, look to our sins. We must also look at the pain and suffering our sin causes. We look back at the suffering of Jesus and at the suffering we have caused others by our sins.

Were we in the crowd that cried "Crucify Him"? See Jesus bruised and beaten. See our Lord fall over and over again under the weight of the cross, under the weight of our sins. Feel the pounding of the nails into Jesus' hands and feet. Did we mock him on the cross? Did we run away and hide when we thought that Jesus was dead, that it was all over?

LENT 1

How many times have we sinned against God and our neighbor? How many people have we hurt by those sins? What can we do to make amends for all the wrong we have done? How do we turn from sin and sorrow to reconciliation and love?

Ultimately, will the weight of our sins drive us to our knees? Will we cry out in pain and in humiliation as we find ourselves at Jesus' feet begging for mercy just as the thief hanging beside him did? Now is the time to repent and turn to God. We are standing in the shadow of the cross.

Almighty and everlasting God, you hate nothing you have made and forgive the sins of all who are penitent: Create and make in us new and contrite hearts, that we, worthily lamenting our sins and acknowledging our wretchedness, may obtain of you, the God of all mercy, perfect remission and forgiveness; through Jesus Christ our Lord.

Ash Wednesday Liturgy, *Book of Common Prayer*, 264

Dear Jesus, as we remember your passion and death as well as the sins that caused your suffering, forgive us, Lord, forgive us. *Amen.*

Thursday, following Ash Wednesday

In The Garden

In preparation for his final hours Jesus spent some time in prayer. Jesus went to a quiet spot, a favorite place of his to pray—the Garden of Gethsemane. No, it was not a place to escape from what lay before him, and Jesus knew that. "Now Judas, who betrayed him, also knew the place, because Jesus often met there with his disciples." (John 18:2) But at least he would have some time for prayer before the final drama of his life began.

Jesus prayed earnestly to his Father, even asking that the heavy burden of what he was about to go through could be lifted from him. How difficult it must have been to face the terrible ordeal that lay before him! But Jesus was steadfast; he accepted the will of his Father. "Father, if you are willing, remove this cup from me; yet, not my will but yours be done." (Luke 22:42) Luke's gospel also says, "an angel from heaven appeared to him and gave him strength." (vs. 43)

When Jesus had finished praying he would have felt that he was properly prepared to face his accusers and all that awaited him. Jesus would also have known that the Spirit of God would be with him in all that he faced. He was now prepared to face his time of trial. "See, the hour is at hand, and the Son of Man is betrayed into the hands of sinners. Get up, let us be going. See, my betrayer is at hand." (Matthew 26: 45-46)

We do well to follow the example of Jesus, especially when we are facing a time of trial. A faithful prayer life is important and especially valuable during stressful times. Prayer helps us to collect our thoughts and calms our spirit. Through prayer we are in direct communication with God, presenting our petitions and fears, just as Jesus did. Our heavenly Father hears our prayers and answers them as he knows best. We receive strength and encouragement through the Holy Spirit to face whatever God's plan is for us.

Do not worry about anything, but in everything by prayer and supplication with thanksgiving let your requests be made known to God.

Philippians 4:6

Jesus, Help us to develop a prayer life such as yours, seeking out the Father for counsel and support, especially in times of trial. *Amen.*

Friday following Ash Wednesday

Betrayal

Why did Judas betray Jesus? Matthew's gospel indicates that money was the motive. "Then one of the twelve, who was called Judas Iscariot, went to the chief priests and said, 'What will you give me if I betray him to you?' They paid him thirty pieces of silver. And from that moment he began to look for an opportunity to betray him." (Matthew 26:14-16)

Was financial gain Judas' only motive? Had he lost faith that Jesus was the Messiah? Was he afraid that his association with Jesus might put his own life in danger? We do not know. We only know that Judas betrayed his friend and Master.

Betrayal is a very personal act because it damages or destroys relationships. Trust is violated. Betrayal occurs between friends and family members, employees betray their employers, and citizens may betray their country.

There are many kinds of betrayals. A friend, family member or co-worker shares a confidence. Not even intending to hurt anyone the information is passed on to another. Sometimes no harm is done; other times grievous harm is done. Betrayal can mean the loss of a friend. It can also mean the loss of a job or a life.

Today we also hear about betrayals by roommates who post intimate and/or embarrassing actions of another person online. We also read about websites that share information that is considered confidential. Consumers have been betrayed by banks. Children have faced the ultimate betrayal at the hands of trusted authority figures.

Some acts seen as betrayals may have redeeming merit as when an employee reveals company activity that is illegal or may be harming others. This has happened to financial companies who are working to defraud their clients and chemical companies who are polluting the environment. However, these kinds of betrayal usually mean making a choice between betraying personal and moral values and betraying a company or employer. What might be seen as betrayal may ultimately be an action taken for the greater good. Thoughtful and prayerful discernment is needed before such action is taken.

Careful consideration in advance of any word or deed that may betray another and the consequence of such actions is not only appropriate but can prevent much heartache and harm. Sin is often prevented when contemplation and prayer proceeds action. Betrayal is not an action that can be undone.

Judas came to realize that the betrayal of Jesus meant an innocent man's death. "When Judas, his betrayer, saw that Jesus was condemned, he repented and brought back the thirty pieces of silver to the chief priests and the elders. He said, 'I have sinned by betraying innocent blood.'" (Matthew 27:3-4)

Jesus, you know what it was like to be betrayed. Help us to consider carefully the consequences of our actions before we consider committing the sin of betrayal. *Amen.*

Saturday, following Ash Wednesday

The Accused

Jesus, the chief priests had only false witnesses to testify against you. "Now the chief priests and the whole council were looking for false testimony against Jesus so that they might put him to death, but they found none, though many false witnesses came forward." (Matthew 26:59-60) You responded with silence to your accusers.

When it was Pilate's turn to question you, you still had little to say. Perhaps this was your way of acknowledging this step was only a formality. Perhaps it was your way of not recognizing Pilate's earthly authority. Then Pilate said to you "Do you refuse to speak to me? Do you not know that I have power to release you, and power to crucify you?" (John 19:10) And you replied, "You would have no power over me unless it had been given you from above." (John 19:11)

When Pilate brought you out before the people, was it hard to stand there before the Jews and hear the cries of rejection and condemnation? Did you look out among the people for a friendly face? Where were those who had followed you from town to town? Where were the five thousand who you fed the fishes and loaves? Were these the same people that such a short time before had spread their cloaks on the road to Jerusalem before you and shouted "Hosanna," and even called you "the King of Israel" (John 12:13)?

The crowd was stirred up by the temple leadership who had been scheming for some time to have you killed. It was easy to turn the mob against you. "Crucify him! Crucify him!" The people rejected you; the course was set.

So then, putting away falsehood, let all of us speak the truth to our neighbours, for we are members of one another.

Ephesians 4:25

Jesus, may I never bear false witness against you. When I cry out on Palm Sunday, "Crucify him," may it be only to remind myself that you died for my sins and for the sins of the whole world. Jesus, have mercy on me a sinner. *Amen.*

Collect For The First Sunday In Lent

Almighty God, whose blessed Son was led by the Spirit to be tempted by Satan: Make speed to help thy servants who are assaulted by manifold temptations; and, as thou knowest their several infirmities, let each one find thee mighty to save; through Jesus Christ, thy Son, our Lord, who liveth and reigneth with thee and the Holy Spirit, one God, now and forever. Amen

****

We are always tempted. There is no getting around it. Look at the way Jesus was tempted. First he was offered bread. Don't we love our bread and our drink and our sweets and our....And we suffer for those sins! Oh, how we suffer for those sins of excess, of gluttony! We go on diets and we say we won't ever eat so much again. But we are weak and we are tempted and we fall time and time again.

Satan tempted Jesus "to throw yourself down," a challenge to prove himself as the "real" Son of God. Don't we test God (and others) this way, too? "If you really loved me...." "God, I know you will do this for me." We fall so easily into the pattern of believing that we know what is best for us. We trust ourselves more than we trust God.

Satan had more tricks in his bag. "Fall down and worship me." Think of all the things we worship and lust after: money, power, fame, etc., etc. Think of all the sin and evil we do to have those things. Oh, get behind us, Satan, for our Lord and God is the only one worthy of our full praise and worship.

Dear Gracious and merciful God, let each one of us be found savable. God, you do know "our manifold sins and wickedness, which from time to time we have most grievously have committed by thought word and deed, against that divine majesty." (Confession of Sin, Holy Eucharist I, *Book of Common Prayer,* 331) May the promise of salvation, the gift of your Son, your all-encompassing love for us be the hope and truth for us that, though we are all sinners equally, we also share equally in the redemption of our souls through the passion and death of our Lord, Jesus Christ.

Please send your Spirit to us just as you did Jesus so that even as we are led into temptation we are also given strength through the Spirit to resist temptation. Just as you know our weakest moments and our deepest darkness you also know our hope is in you, now and forever. *Amen.*

THE FIRST STATION

Jesus is condemned to death

But they shouted all the more, 'Crucify him!'

Mark 15:14

Monday, First Week of Lent

Jesus Is Condemned To Death

Jesus is condemned. He is one of the damned. "Why? Because he is different. He is black, and blacks are dangerous. He is gay and gays are perverts.... He is a refugee and refugees are a threat to our economy." (*Walk with Jesus: Stations of the Cross*, 1990, Henri Nouwen, 9) Jesus is the face of all the condemned.

Jesus loved the "other." He loved the Samaritan and the tax collector. He broke bread with those whom others shunned. He upset the comfortableness of the synagogue leaders with his proclamations of new beginnings and salvation for all. His teaching and preaching needed to be stopped lest the people turn against the leaders in the Temple. And so he was condemned. "Crucify him," they all said.

We, too, are condemned. We are condemned as Jesus' disciples were, and as all Christians are. We are condemned by our decision to follow a crucified prophet, because we choose to believe that he lived and died for us. We have this crazy belief that he was resurrected from the dead and lives again just as we will also live with him in heaven some day. We believe this was all done out of love, simply out of God's love for his creation, his children.

What kind of craziness is this? Loving the black and the gay and the refugee? This is the craziness that Jesus taught us. Loving our neighbor as ourselves *and* as God loves us. When we do reach out in love and compassion to all our brothers and sisters in Christ, we are condemned. We are condemned by a world that does not want to hear that we are all neighbors.

We are condemned because we dare to speak out the truth and say that the black man and the lesbian and the immigrant are part of our family; that we are all brothers and sisters in Christ. We welcome those with AIDS and those who speak other languages. We open our doors and our hearts to the sick, the hungry and the needy. The world does not understand this; it does not understand us. So we are condemned like Jesus because we do not follow the world, we are apart from the world.

Jesus says we are not a part of that world. "Because you do not belong to the world, but I have chosen you out of the world—therefore the world hates you." (John 15:19) So we are condemned as Jesus was condemned. We are condemned to pick up our cross and follow him.

Jesus, I pray that I will always choose your just judgment of my failures to love all my brothers and sisters over the condemnation of the world. *Amen.*

Tuesday, First Week of Lent

In The Face Of Death

The road to Calvary is a journey toward death. Facing death never comes easy. Whether it is the death of a loved one or that of our loving Lord, there are no easy answers.

I had gone to Henderson, Nevada, to help my son cope with his father's death. My ex-husband's suicide was a shock for all of us and my son had no one else to be there and support him. We had opened all the windows and kept the bedroom door shut, but the apartment had been closed up for days and the smell of death was still overpowering.

I finally entered the room to begin the task of clearing out the bloody evidence—something I did not want my son to do although he had insisted on seeing it. The wall behind the bed was covered with blood that had run down onto the carpet. The bed sheets were splattered, and in some places soaked with blood, and mixed in pieces of the brains and bones—and the black curly hair of my ex-husband.

Some people say suicide is cowardly; others say it is a courageous act. Many call it sin. Simple explanations do not answer the deeper questions. Oh, we knew, and found out more, about the gambling and the debts, the deception and the fraud. Suicide seems to me to be a great, deep cry of physical, mental, emotional, spiritual pain from lost children of our loving God. So he ends their unending pain by bringing them home.

During the torturous hours waiting for my sister (acting as our attorney) to call and tell me the Henderson police had confirmed

John's death, many thoughts and questions raced through my mind. John was dead. He had killed himself. Why did he do it? Why didn't he reach out for help? Now, many years later, the thoughts still come occasionally. I still have questions; I still have no answers. But I do know that God was with us during that dark time when we faced John's death, and his continuing presence helps those of us left behind to cope. One of the first things I said to my son was that I believed that his father was no longer suffering; that he was in heaven with our Lord.

Lord Jesus, because of your death and resurrection, death has no dominion over us. Thanks be to God. *Amen.*

Wednesday, First Week of Lent

A Good Death

When my friend Phil was dying of AIDS, I was able to spend his last hours with him. For much of three days I stayed by his side, rubbing his head, whispering reassurance to him, promising that I would not let go of his hand until Jesus took him by the hand to take him home. Many people came to say goodbye. There was a lot of praying and singing. Phil died a "beautiful" death, surrounded by loved ones.

The last hours of Jesus' life were very different. Most of his friends were in hiding, fearing the wrath of the Roman government or the Jewish religious leaders. His mother had to stand helplessly by, watching him suffer, watching him die. Every minute of his final hours was spent in pain and suffering.

In my work as a chaplain I have seen people suffer a great deal at the time of their death. I have been with people dying who had no one else at their side. However, the amount of suffering a person bears, or the number of people in attendance, does not represent that person's preparedness for death. Although Jesus suffered greatly, and may have seemed to be abandoned, God was with him at the time of his death. I believe this was true of my friend, Phil, as well.

Preparation for death means examining our lives, confessing our sins, and making amends when we can do so. This is in preparation to stand before Jesus, our judge. Preparing for death does not mean there will be no fear of pain or of the process of dying. Preparation does mean that we accept death as a transition to a new life; that we are prepared to meet our Lord. We know that heaven awaits us.

Not everyone gets the opportunity to prepare for death. Many of us do not know that death awaits us in a sudden accident, a heart attack, etc. So preparation for death needs to be ongoing; it needs to be a part of our life just as Jesus spent his entire life preparing for his death. If we live every day of our lives prepared to die, then we will have no fear of being unprepared for death.

> *Death has nothing terrible which life has not made so. A faithful Christian life in this world is the best preparation for the next.*
>
> Byron Edwards

Dear Heavenly Father, Help us to have hearts always ready to receive Jesus, our merciful and righteous judge, so that when the hour of our death comes we will welcome his call to come home. *Amen.*

That we may end our lives in faith and hope, without suffering and without reproach, let us pray to the Lord.

Lord, have mercy.

> Prayers of the People, Form I,
> *Book of Common Prayer,* 385

THE SECOND STATION

Jesus takes up his cross

He humbled himself
and became obedient to the point of death
— even death on a cross.

Philippians 2:8

Thursday, First Week of Lent

Jesus Takes Up His Cross

We adore you, Oh Christ, and we bless you:
Because by your holy cross you have redeemed the world.

The time has come, Jesus. The Roman soldiers lift up the heavy crossbeam, place it on your shoulders, and force you to move ahead. You stagger under that tremendous weight; you are weakened by the beatings. What a cruel form of punishment and death. You are forced to carry to the place of your death the cross on which they will crucify you. Still, you say nothing. You accept the burden. The weight of that crossbeam could not compare to the weight of all of the sins of the world that you are carrying with you.

You are obedient to the will of your Father. You accept this cross, this heavy weight of sin, and you accept it willingly. "Am I not to drink the cup that the Father has given me?" (John 18:11) That is the mission for which you were born into this world. Your death would pay the price for all our sins. Jesus, out of divine love for us, you, in all your wounded and betrayed humanity, carried this cross to Calvary and died upon it.

What have we done to make that cross so heavy? Every sin we commit against the will of the Father adds weight to that cross. Big sins, little sins, they are all sins against God. Jesus, please forgive the pain we cause you by our sins.

What can we do to ease the burden and the pain of our sins? We can confess our sins and repent them. We can ask for forgiveness and seek reconciliation. We can do penance and make restitution when possible. When a sinner turns from sin and returns to God all of heaven rejoices. The weight of that heavy cross of sin becomes lighter and our own souls feel lighter. We are restored to a right relationship with God. Going forward we can resolve to avoid sin and follow the will of God by taking up our cross and following Jesus.

This one event of the cross of Christ is a final revelation of the character and the consequences of human sin and of the wonder and sacrifice of divine love.

Alan M. Stibbs

Jesus, not even all my love and all my obedience to your will can equal the gift that you gave to me upon the cross. May I always repent my sins, return to your light and love, and carry my cross so willingly. *Amen.*

Lift high the cross,
the love of Christ proclaim
'til all the world
adore his sacred name.

Hymn #473
George William Kitchen and
Michael Newbolt, 1916,
The Hymnal 1982

Friday, First Week of Lent

Follow Him

Jesus died on the cross more than two thousand years ago. The Old Testament stories date back much further than that. How do we stay connected to the foundations of our faith when the stories may not seem relevant or even real today? How do we learn and apply these teachings in our world today?

Although crucifixion is not a common practice in our society today, we still have brutal dictatorships and examples of oppressed societies. People are martyred every day for their faith. It is not enough to be aware that prejudice, hatred and cruelty exist. We must speak out about these crimes against humanity. We need to support efforts to bring freedom of religion, equality and justice to all nations of the world.

Lying, cheating, stealing and other sins are committed by people every day just as they were back in the time of Jesus. In our own homes and faith communities we can teach our children about God and Jesus, and stories from the Bible can help children learn the difference between right and wrong. "Show them that your ways give more life than the ways of the world, and that following you is better than chasing after selfish goals." ("For Young Persons," *Book of Common Prayer,* 829)

We can offer times for worship, prayer and study that will confirm and strengthen our faith. We can study the lessons of the Bible and apply them to the realities of our own world. The examples of early Christians can give us positive role models for our own lives.

We can be witnesses to and examples of the mission and ministry of Christ in our world. When we see Christ in others, and act accordingly we are spreading the message of the Bible, and we are becoming Christ-like ourselves. And as we do so we can better understand those ancient teachings from God and can apply them to our own lives.

Yes, our world is different than the world two thousand years ago. but we still struggle with the same issues. Intolerance, hatred and prejudice still prevail. Jesus would still be out here throwing the money-changers out of our temples of greed, he would still be ministering to the poor and the sick; he would still be preaching his ministry of love and reconciliation. For our faith to come alive we need to do what Jesus asked his disciples to do over two thousand years ago—follow him.

Jesus, lead us, as you led over two thousand years ago, to cry out against injustice, to minister to the sick and needy, to love al our brothers and sisters. Lead on, Jesus, lead on. *Amen.*

Saturday, First Week of Lent

The Obedient Child

Jesus is a child of God, the son of God. He was also the child of Mary and of Joseph. Jesus had both a heavenly Father and earthly parents, and he was an obedient son. He brought into this world his love of God and the understanding that he came on a mission: to do the will of his Father in heaven. As the son of Mary and Joseph, Jesus set the example of a devoted and obedient child. "Then he went down with them and came to Nazareth, and was obedient to them." (Luke 2:51)

At the beginning of his ministry, after Jesus was baptized in the Jordan, "A voice from heaven said, 'This is my Son, the Beloved, with whom I am well pleased.'"(Matthew 3:17) Here was God the Father proclaiming his love and approval of his Son. Throughout his life on earth Jesus urged others to follow the example of a Son obedient to a father. "Truly I tell you, unless you change and become like children, you will never enter the kingdom of heaven. Whoever becomes humble like this child is the greatest in the kingdom of heaven. Whoever welcomes one such child in my name welcomes me." (Matthew 18:3-5)

In the Garden of Gethsemane Jesus showed his continuing obedience to the will of his Father: He said, "Abba, Father, for you all things are possible; remove this cup from me; yet, not what I want, but what you want." (Mark 14:36) As Jesus was dying his final thought was of his Father. "Then Jesus, crying with a loud voice, said, 'Father, into your hands I commend my spirit.' Having said this, he breathed his last." (Luke 23:46) Jesus was a child, obedient to the will of the Father, even in his death.

How do we show obedience to our Heavenly Father? As children we are obedient to our parents, just as Jesus was. Through these acts of obedience we learn the importance of following the will of our parents, and our parents and our church teach us to be obedient to God in the same way. As adults we have opportunities to serve God and our fellow human beings just as Jesus did. By these acts of obedience to the will of our Father we express our love of God and his son, Jesus Christ.

Obedience to God is the most infallible evidence of sincere and supreme love to him.

Nathanael Emmons

Father, may we, as your children, show our love by always being Christ-like in our obedience to your will. *Amen.*

Collect For The Second Sunday In Lent

Oh God, whose glory it is always to have mercy: Be gracious to all who have gone astray from thy ways and bring them again with penitent hearts and steadfast faith to embrace and hold fast the unchangeable truth of thy Word, Jesus Christ thy Son; who with thee and the Holy Spirit liveth and reigneth, one God, for ever and ever. Amen.

****

We don't just stray, Lord. We wander off into distant corners of our own universes where we are lord and master. We march to different drummers and guitar players and keyboard artists, so loud they could drown out any heavenly choir. We declare that we have all the answers, know all the truths and understand everything. When we are finished self-congratulating ourselves we turn back to worshipping our electronic world, all that glitters —gold or not, and the fountain of our eternal youth.

Lord, it is hard to hear you in the din. It is hard to see you in the bling and it is hard to feel your presence in this wired world. We are too busy with our phones to feed the hungry, clothe the naked and shelter the homeless. Of course, there are apps for that. We don't even have time for face-to-face time with each other, much less time for our brother or sister. And church—try to remember to turn off your phone before the service, maybe take a peek at texts during the passing of the peace and check for messages during the recessional.

We stray so far away. What can bring us home? Oh, for the

quiet of the sanctuary where God is whispering his sacred words of truth in our hearts. Here we acknowledge that God is Lord and that we offend him by disobedience to his word.

We are lost. Who can bring us home? It is Jesus Christ our Lord who calls upon the Father to breathe his spirit into our hearts and make a shrine for Jesus there. Then we are home.

Oh Gracious God, we pray indeed that you will be merciful to us who have forgotten what it is like to show mercy or to know mercy. By your Spirit show us your ways and your Truth. Teach us to be faithful and obedient to thy will in all ways and all times in the holy name of Jesus Christ our Redeemer. *Amen.*

THE THIRD STATION

Jesus falls the first time

For I am ready to fall,
and my pain is ever with me.

Psalm 38:17

Monday, Second Week of Lent

Jesus Falls The First Time

Jesus, how heavy that crossbeam must have been; how great was your suffering! You were beaten down by the weight and your pain. How hard it must have been to get back up and struggle onward.

Did anyone reach out to help you when you fell? Maybe no one was allowed to do so. Maybe even those who might have wanted to help you were afraid. Perhaps they feared for their own lives.

Jesus, you have called us to carry our own cross, to walk with you as you carry your cross. "Then he said to them all, 'If any want to become my followers, let them deny themselves and take up their cross daily and follow me.'" (Luke 9:23) But the crossbeam you give us to carry is leavened by your love for us. "Take my yoke upon you, and learn from me; for I am gentle and humble in heart, and you will find rest for your souls. For my yoke is easy, and my burden is light." (Matthew 11:29-30)

Jesus, being reminded that you fell, in all you misery and humanness, reminds us that we, too, are prone to falling. The journey is difficult for us, too. We fall daily. But when we do, you are right there by our side, to pick us up, to encourage us, to support us. No matter how bruised and beaten down we are your own sacrifice is reason enough for us to get up and carry on.

Thank you, Jesus, for giving us a cross that you know we can carry. You trust that we will be able to carry our burden, but we also know that you will be right there beside us if we fall.

Knowing that, we, like you, can struggle to our feet.

> *The cross is a picture of violence, yet the key to peace,
> a picture of suffering, yet the key to healing, a picture of
> death, yet the key of life.*
>
> David Watson

Jesus, May the Spirit fill us with the courage that filled you when you had fallen under the weight of our sins. *Amen.*

Tuesday, Second Week of Lent

Please Jesus Get Up

Jesus staggers under the weight of the cross, his body buckles and he falls down. Some people in the crowd gasp; others wince; and his loved ones weep silently. Somewhere in the crowd a little girl peeks out from behind her mother's skirts. She sees that Jesus has fallen and it makes her very sad. She wants to go and help him up, but she knows that would make her mother angry and the soldiers would yell at her.

She doesn't really know why people are being mean to Jesus now. They didn't act that way before and he seemed like such a nice man. One day, after he had talked a long time and everybody was hungry, he gave them all some fish and bread to eat. It was good.

Another time while her mother was listening to Jesus, he beckoned to her. She hesitated. She was kind of shy and not sure that she wanted to go, but her mother pushed her forward. He hugged her and let her sit on his lap while he was talking. She liked that.

Now she sees him lying there in the dirt with that big heavy piece of wood on top of him and she feels really sorry for him. His head and face are all bloody and his clothes are bloody too. He looks like he has been hurt really bad. Why don't the soldiers just go away and leave him alone?

She scoots a little bit closer without getting too far away from her mother, and she squats down near Jesus, looking closely at him. Just then he turns his head and looks at her. He doesn't

33

really smile at her. He probably hurts too much to do that. But he gives her a nice look, like he remembers her.

Suddenly the soldiers begin whipping Jesus and kicking at him, telling him to get up. He tries to get up but she can see he is having a very hard time. He is still looking at her, and just as her mother pulls her away, she whispers to him, "Please Jesus get up. Can you go just a little more—for me?"

Sweet, sweet Jesus, can you get up? Can you go just a little bit further—for me? *Amen.*

Wednesday, Second Week of Lent

Life and Death

I will not just live my life. I will not just spend my life.
I will invest my life.

Helen Adams Keller

Life is easy enough to live casually or recklessly. It is much more difficult to invest one's life in something that is truly worthwhile. God challenges us to live a life invested in him and in his love for us.

Jesus invested his life and his death in us. We surely can invest our life in him. Then our life after death will be assured.

Life can be worth the energy it takes to live it only if
it is governed by something that is stronger than death.

J. Neville Ward

That which governs our life should be the commandments of God and the example of Jesus Christ. We know that the love of God is more powerful than death. These should be the rules of our life.

Life is filled with meaning as soon as Jesus Christ
enters into it.

Bishop Stephen Charles Neill

When Christ is the center of our life we are focused on him and his love in turn is focused on us. Much is accomplished by this relationship, and much is gained. God is good to us.

LENT 13

Take care of your life and the Lord will take care of your death.

George Whitefield

Jesus has promised us a place in heaven. We have only to live a life worthy of that place reserved and eternity is guaranteed. That makes life something important to nurture and care for; it is our ticket to eternity.

Jesus, you had a choice. You chose death so that we could have eternal life. Each of us has a choice as well. We can choose a life that ends in death or we can choose the kind of life that will lead to an eternity with you in heaven. The choice is ours.

Jesus, may I always choose you and the life that your Father has chosen for me. *Amen.*

THE FOURTH STATION

Jesus meets his afflicted mother

You will conceive in your womb and bear a son,
and you will name him Jesus.

Thursday, Second Week of Lent

Jesus meets his afflicted mother

There is no biblical evidence that Mary was in the crowd that lined the path to Calvary, although John's account of the passion clearly has her stationed under the cross. "Meanwhile, standing near the cross of Jesus were his mother, and his mother's sister, Mary the wife of Clopas, and Mary Magdalene." (John 19: 25) It seems likely that Mary was very close at hand. It is not hard to imagine her standing there, watching her son make his tortuous way to his death.

He looks up and sees you standing there, so helpless, so full of grief. He sees all his suffering reflected in your motherly eyes. There is nothing that either of you can do but look at each other, and share your pain.

Still it must have been some comfort to him to know that you were there, to know that someone cared. How you must have longed to hold him in your arms, to comfort him. You surely must have wanted to do so, but dared not even touch him.

You had been warned when Jesus was presented at the Temple that "a sword will pierce your own soul too." (Luke 2:35) Of course, at the time you could have no way of knowing that his life would be ending in this way. The angel Gabriel told you that the child you were to bear would "reign over the house of Jacob for ever, and of his kingdom there will be no end." (Luke 1:33) This could not possibly seem like a fitting end for one destined to be a king. In your anguish you must have been so confused, unable to make any sense of this.

Yet you were faithful and loving. You did not run away. You did not abandon your son. Whatever he suffered you were going to be right there, suffering with him. He did not abandon you. He made sure you were taken care of after his death. "When Jesus saw his mother and the disciple whom he loved standing beside her, he said to his mother, 'Woman, here is your son.' Then he said to the disciple, 'Here is your mother.' And from that hour the disciple took her into his own home." (John 19:26-27)

Mary, my heavenly mother, be with me when I am suffering and in pain. Gaze on me with your comforting eyes when I am in sore distress. Please ask your son to bless me. *Amen.*

Friday, Second Week of Lent

Mother

Jesus raised his head and looked toward the crowd. He struggled to focus his weary, blood-shot eyes. Standing a bit apart from the crowd he saw his mother, head slightly bowed, hands clasped together as though in prayer.

"Mother." The word would not come forth. Jesus was too exhausted to speak. He looked lovingly at his mother and thought, "What can I say to you? I have no strength left to say what I would like to say. You know that I love you. I am so sorry that you have to suffer through all of this."

Mary seemed to hear those words of love and raised her head. She looked directly at Jesus. Their eyes connected, passing the kind of look that is between mother and son. Mary smiled a brief sad smile, reached out her hand tentatively and then withdrew it, clasping her hands together again. She slowly lowered her head. Tears slipped own her cheeks.

Jesus lowered his head, too, shifted the weight of the cross and struggled forward. As he passed by his mother he looked at her again but said nothing. The love and grief he felt for his mother tore at his heart.

Inside his heart reached out to her again and said, "Goodbye, mother. Thank you for all your care and love. Thank you for being so patient and steadfast."

Jesus knew the pain would be ending for him soon, but that his mother would live with those terrible memories for the rest of her life. "Some day," he thought, "when all of this is long past, I will come and take you home to be with me and my Father in heaven forever. You will no longer suffer but will be crowned queen of heaven."

Jesus, what great love your mother had for you and you for her. May our hearts be filled with the same love for you. *Amen.*

Saturday, Second Week of Lent

Mary's Faith And Devotion

An article from the Catholic Encyclopedia on the "Way of the Cross," states that "tradition asserts that the Blessed Virgin used to visit daily the scenes of Christ's passion." ("Way of the Cross," *Catholic Encyclopedia* http://www.newadvent.org/cathen/15569a.htm) I had never heard this before, even through all my years of Catholic school or in Sunday School or Bible classes. I have thought about this and wondered about it for a while.

My question has been, why? Just on a purely human level I would ask why Mary would continue to torture herself by following again and again the steps leading to her son's death. However, the bigger question that presents itself to me is one that is more theological in nature. If Mary believed that her son was the Messiah, and that he died and was raised from the dead, then why would she feel a need to focus on his death?

We do not know from Holy Scripture if Jesus appeared to Mary after his death. According to the Act of the Apostles, Mary was with the apostles after Jesus' death. "All these were constantly devoting themselves to prayer, together with certain women, including Mary, the mother of Jesus." (Acts 1:14) This definitely seems to indicate that Mary was among those first Christians who believed in the resurrection of Jesus.

Certainly a reason for us to follow the way of the cross is to make more real to us the passion and death of Jesus. Mary had no reason to do so; it must have been more than real enough to her. So, if Mary did indeed take this sad journey daily what might have been her reason? Was it to help other Christians in their faith in the risen Christ? Was it to show devotion to her son?

Mary's humble acceptance of the divine will is the starting point of the story of the redemption of the human race from sin.

Alan Richardson

Jesus, I ponder your passion and death and your mother's passion, too. There are no easy answers. Help my sorrowing heart to understand and to seek forgiveness for all the pain and suffering I have caused you both. *Amen.*

Collect for the Third Sunday in Lent

Almighty God, who seest that we have no power of ourselves to help ourselves: Keep us both outwardly in our bodies and inwardly in our souls that we may be defended from all adversities which may happen to the body, and from all evil thoughts which may assault and hurt the soul; through Jesus Christ our Lord, who liveth and reigneth with thee and the Holy Spirit, one God, for ever and ever. Amen.

****

We humans are weak. We are not able to protect ourselves from sickness of the body, mind and spirit. Even with all our modern medicine we get sick, suffer and die. Our mental health is fragile too, buffeted by grief, depression, and sicknesses of the mind.

God knows our weaknesses and hears our prayers for protection from sickness, pain, and suffering. The Spirit abides with us in our illnesses, watching over us until we are restored to health. If it is the will of God to give to us the ultimate healing, Jesus is ready to take us home.

God also sends his Spirit upon us, to help protect us from evil thoughts. Such bad thoughts may seek to drive a wedge between us and God, tempting us to follow the ways of the devil instead of the will of the Lord. These evil thoughts corrupt the purity of our souls and lead to sin and corruption.

Heavenly Father, as our creator you know the fragileness of our bodies, our minds and our spirits. Send your Spirit to dwell within us and protect us from all bodily harm. Heal us when we fall ill and restore us to your heavenly kingdom when our bodies ultimately fail us.

We pray for protection from all assaults of the mind. Protect us from mental illness and from the power of the devil to corrupt our minds. Satan has no power over us when Jesus places himself and his cross between us and the working of evil in our lives.

Lord, Please kindly save us from all ill health of body, mind and spirit. Let not evil thoughts hold sway in these temples of the Holy Spirit. And may your grace and blessings be upon us in our final hours. *Amen.*

THE FIFTH STATION

The cross is laid on
Simon of Cyrene

And they laid the cross on him

Luke 23:26

Monday, Third Week of Lent

The Cross Is Laid On Simon Of Cyrene

Simon, the gospels seem to imply you played an unwilling role in the crucifixion of Jesus. "As they led him away, they seized a man, Simon of Cyrene, who was coming from the country, and they laid the cross on him, and made him carry it behind Jesus." (Luke 23:26). Some of your family history is mentioned in Mark, perhaps linking you to an associate of Paul, Rufus. "It was Simon of Cyrene, the father of Alexander and Rufus." (Mark15:21) The little we do know is that you helped our Lord carry his cross. What an honor, what a privilege, even though you may not have thought so at the time, struggling under that heavy weight. Probably you did not even really know what was going on.

I wonder if we know this small bit of your story because you told others about your role or maybe someone who witnessed the crucifixion of Jesus saw you there. Was it with pride you told your story: "Yes, I helped him," or did you try to explain away your part by telling how the soldiers grabbed you and forced the heavy crossbeam on your shoulders? We know nothing more about you. We can only speculate.

Maybe Jesus was able to give you a look of appreciation. Maybe you could sense his relief. I hope you did feel some sense of pride in helping to relieve the suffering of this condemned man. Here was an opportunity for you to help your brother, to help him carry his heavy burden. I believe that Jesus returned the favor. What I believe is that at the hour of your death Jesus was waiting there with open arms to carry you home.

How many times does the innocent bystander become the hero? How often are we offered the opportunity to serve others? That is part of God's plan; brothers and sisters serving one another. We who consider ourselves Christians are called to serve our fellow human beings in the name of Jesus just as Simeon of Cyrene was able to serve Jesus during this terrible time of the suffering and death of our Lord.

Thank you, God for all of those who serve us, and all who serve in the name of Jesus. *Amen.*

Tuesday, Third Week of Lent

Turn Back, Turn Away

That sounds like the easiest thing to do. When the going gets tough just turn back, give up and retreat. And when you are faced with something or someone to difficult to handle, just turn away. This makes for a comfortable life, avoiding changes and challenges, confrontation and commitment.

What if Jesus had "turned back" on us? What if Jesus had decided we were not worth saving when he was in the Garden of Gethsemane thinking of what lay ahead? What if he had given up on humankind, left us in our sins; turned away and took off for parts unknown? Who would have blamed him?

We know that Jesus was not like that. He did not turn his back or walk away. He met his challengers face to face. He was firm and sometimes very stern, especially when people were lying or denying the Father, but he spoke the truth with love.

Jesus wanted us to have a better life. He was sorry that his message was not accepted. It would have been so much easier if people had accepted him as the Messiah, if they had accepted his message of truth and love.

That was not the way it was meant to be. God had to prove to us just how much he loved us in the only way that we would really understand. Jesus would have to make the ultimate sacrifice, he would have to die. And then, when he was raised from the dead, some people would believe.

So Jesus did not turn his back on us; he did not turn away.

He rose to meet the challenge and the sacrifice with grace and courage. And we must be always thankful that he did.

> *The Christian character is the flower of which sacrifice is the seed.*
>
> Fr. Andrew

Jesus, thank you so much that you did not turn back, turn away. You did not abandon us in our sins. May our hearts be always thankful for your great sacrifice. *Amen.*

Wednesday, Third Week of Lent

Right Place, Right Time

Simon of Cyrene may very well have felt he was caught in the wrong place and the wrong time. How many of us have felt that way? We feel trapped sometimes or at least awkward at the time and the place we may find ourselves in. We feel we are not the right persons for the particular job or task; someone else could do it better. Our time is being wasted. We would be better off spending our time doing something else, or doing the task at some other time. So we may find ourselves trying to get out of what we feel we are being forced or coerced to do, or doing the job half-heartedly, or not at all.

Does this sound like how Jesus approached his earthly mission? From the time he was a boy until his final hours on earth, Jesus not only seemed to be in the right place at the right time, but also proclaimed that to others. When found by his anxious parents in the Temple, Jesus said, "Did you not know that I must be in my Father's house?" (Luke 2:49) As he breathed his dying breath on the cross Jesus said, "It is finished."(John 19:30) Jesus was in just the right place at the right time.

I believe that Simon of Cyrene did not shirk from the calling to duty. He accepted the call to serve our Lord, just as Jesus obeyed the will of his Father. Simon was in the right place and the right time.

Focusing on those tasks we are called by God to do, just as Jesus did, can give us a definite sense of purpose and helps us to feel that we are a part of God's plan. Then we can see we are that one person who is the right one to accomplish God's work at that time and in that place. And we can say as Mary said, "Here am I, the servant of the Lord." (Luke 1:38)

Here am I, Lord. Is it I, Lord?
I have heard you calling in the night.
I will go, Lord, if you lead me.
I will hold your people in my heart.

Daniel L. Schutte, 1981

Dear God, thank you for people like Simon of Cyrene who answer your call just as Jesus did. May we always be ready to serve you. *Amen.*

THE SIXTH STATION

A woman wipes the face of Jesus

A great number of the people followed him,
and among them were women.

Luke 23:27

A Woman Wipes The Face Of Jesus

Who is this woman who wipes the face of Jesus? There is no mention of her in the gospels. Some call her Veronica. If she is one of the women of Jerusalem that Jesus addresses, why is she given a name and not the others?

According to the *Catholic Encyclopedia*, "Veronica is a name popularly given to one of the women who accompanied Christ to Calvary. 'Veronica' is an abbreviation of 'vera icon' (true image), and the woman now called Veronica is said to have offered a towel to Christ, on which he left the imprint of his face." This is a possible explanation of how the name "Veronica" became part of the legend. There are conflicting claims about the existence of the cloth used and who might be in possession of it. ("Veronica," *Catholic Encyclopedia*, http://www.newadvent. org/cathen/15362a.htm)

In one version of the legend of Veronica she was a pious (and perhaps) wealthy woman of Jerusalem who felt pity for Jesus and offered him her veil to wipe his face. Her name was Seraphia and her husband was a member of the Sanhedran. That might explain why the Roman soldiers allowed her to approach Jesus. ("Veronica Wipes the Face of Jesus," the *Virtual Museum of the Cross*, http://www.freelaunch.com/museum/cross6.html)

It would certainly have been a kind and gracious act for a woman to step forward from the crowd and offer her veil to wipe Jesus' face. When others stood by just watching or bemoaning Jesus' fate, she was probably risking her reputation (and that of her husband) by making this courageous gesture. This simple act is to be remembered more for the compassion shown for Jesus than any relic that may have been the consequence of her action. By her action Veronica exemplified Jesus' teaching of loving one another as God loves us.

Would we have the courage to step forward at such a time? Do we take risks in order to serve or only offer assistance when we feel safe or when it is popular or profitable to do so? Do we need to know that others see or hear of our generosity of spirit or can we act out of simple and humble loving kindness?

Jesus, may our acts of kindness and generosity towards others reflect the spirit of this woman called Veronica. *Amen.*

Friday, Third Week of Lent

Close To God

Inside of each of us is an emptiness completed only by God. What we seek is total union with God. This connection will be complete only when we are reunited with God in heaven, but that longing haunts us here on earth.

We seek to be close to God in worship at church on Sunday or during our daily prayers or meditations. We study the word of God to understand his teaching, and we reach out to him in prayer and praise and hymn. Although we may experience fleeting moments of ecstasy these are but glimpses of the glory.

We experience brief moments of union with God through the sacrament of the Holy Eucharist. Jesus gave us this gift of his body and blood so that we would have a foretaste of that heavenly banquet. Even this physical and spiritual experience of God within allows only momentary intimacy with God. We hunger for so much more.

What we may forget is that the way we can get closest to God is through the cross of our Lord. Jesus, dying on the cross, was in total union with and in complete obedience to his heavenly Father. It is in that perfect state of divine grace that we can be closest to God on earth.

We cannot transport ourselves back two thousand years and help Jesus carry the cross as Simon of Cyrene did. And that is not what is expected of us. God has given each of us our own cross to bear. We may not recognize our own personal cross for what it really is, but that will be revealed to us in time through prayer and faith.

Reach out now for the cross that Jesus is giving you. Join him on his way to Calvary. It is the way of truth and love. Jesus is the way to God.

Draw near to God, and he will draw near to you.

James 4:8

Jesus, May I accept my cross willingly and follow you faithfully seeking always to be closer to you. *Amen.*

Saturday, Third Week of Lent

The Palm Of His Hands

It is hard to think of the searing pain of nails being pounded into Jesus' hand, and the further agony as he hung dying on the cross. Those were strong hands, good hands, loving hands. Those were the hands that Mary held when Jesus was a child. Those were hands that worked hard learning the trade of a carpenter in Joseph's shop. Those were the hands that offered the touch of healing as Jesus ministered to others. Those were the hands that blessed the bread and wine and changed it into Jesus' own body and blood. Those were the hands clasped in prayer as Jesus prayed in his darkest hour in the Garden of Gethsemane.

Sometimes in our own darkness and misery we would do well to think on the hands of Jesus, those hands that loved much and suffered much. Sometimes we feel truly alone with no hands to hold us, no words of comfort. We long for some human touch, to know that someone cares.

I have a prayer card that shows an angel embracing and ministering to Jesus in the Garden of Gethsemane. It is clear in this picture that our Lord is receiving great comfort from that angel sent from God. Likewise we are comforted by God in our times of greatest need. I am comforted at times just by looking at that picture. It reassures me that God is there for me.

God gives us angels to watch over us and protect us. The Spirit is present always for comfort and counsel. Jesus walks with us, indeed carries us when our burdens are too great for us to bear alone.

Our loving God has told us he will not abandon us. "I will not forget you. See, I have inscribed you on the palms of my hands." (Isaiah 49:15-16) On those wounded, bleeding hands each and every one of our names was inscribed. Jesus died for each and every one of us. He did not forsake us; he will never forsake us.

So in the darkness think of the hands of Jesus. Feel those hands holding you and caressing you, caring for you when you feel so much alone. And when you gaze upon Jesus on the cross look at those hands with your name inscribed upon them—and give him thanks and praise.

Dear Lord, thanks so much for caring for me, and for loving me so much. *Amen.*

Collect For The Fourth Sunday In Lent

Gracious Father, whose blessed Son, Jesus Christ, came down from heaven to be the true bread which giveth life to the world: Evermore give us this bread, that he may live in us, and we in him; who liveth and reigneth with thee and the Holy Spirit, one God, now and for ever. Amen.

****

Bread. It is the most basic of foods. Bread is made of the most basic of elements: water and grain. There are many forms of bread and many ways to make it. Bread is known to have nourished human bodies from the earliest biblical times; we consume bread today as our forefathers did then.

Jesus took this most common of foods and elevated it to a unique status. He blessed this bread; broke it and it became his body. That body was given to us, shared with us, died for us. Through these acts Jesus became bread for us, the bread of life, true bread.

I am the living bread that came down from heaven. Whoever eats of this bread will live for ever; and the bread that I will give for the life of the world is my flesh.

John 6:51

Every time that bread is blessed and broken we have the opportunity not only to share the bread but also to partake in the sacrifice of Jesus Christ. By the breaking of that bread we are broken and by the gift of the sacrifice of the body we are healed and made whole, restored once again.

For as often as you eat this bread and drink the cup, you proclaim the Lord's death until he comes.

1 Corinthians 11:26

Any ordinary bread can nourish our bodies. This bread has the unique ability to nourish our souls, to give us life. That is why it is called true bread. We may not understand the mystery of this bread but we know that our spirits long for this bread, we hunger for it.

Dear God, we thank you for the gift of the true bread of life, you Son and our Savior, Jesus Christ. The remembrance of his gift of love for us is so precious. May we always come to the table of our Lord having made careful preparation to receive this sacred gift. May we always celebrate the breaking of the bread and the receiving of the body of our Lord with due reverence and adoration.

Through this sacrament we are made one in Jesus and he in us. Our souls are nourished, our spirits fed. We are restored to life in Christ as heirs of the kingdom of God. This bread not only nourishes but strengthens us for service, Lord. May we always leave the table of our Lord refreshed and renewed and ready to serve in the most holy name of Jesus. *Amen.*

THE SEVENTH STATION

Jesus falls a second time

The Lord upholds all who are falling,
and raises up all who are bowed down.

Psalm 145:14

Monday, Fourth Week of Lent

Jesus Falls A Second Time

Jesus falls again. We all fall, again and again and again and again. What does it take to get back up when we fall over and over, when we **fail** over and over? What it takes is the image of a Savior who fell, and got back up again and fell again and who got back up again.

How did he do that? How did he pick up his face that was ground into the dust and stones, his head crowned with thorns? How did he push his battered body off the ground and stagger to his feet? How did he find the strength to pick up the cross? How did he find the will to go on?

"Not my will but yours be done." (Luke 22:42) It was an act of will; an act of obedience. Jesus' obedience to the Father was the obedience of a perfect son. All that the Father asked him to do he would do, no matter what the personal sacrifice.

> *Obedience means marching right on whether we feel like it or not.*
>
> Dwight Lyman (D.L.) Moody

When we fall into sin, when we fail to follow the will of the Father, we must look to the image of that son, loving and obedient to his Father. We must summon all our courage to follow the will of the Father, to be obedient to his will. We must follow the example of Jesus, the obedient son.

> *It is a vain thought to flee from the work that God appoints us, for the sake of finding a greater blessing,*

instead of seeking it where alone it is to be found—in loving obedience.

George Eliot

Heavenly Father, Teach us obedience to your perfect will in all we say and do for it is through that obedience that we grow in faith and love. *Amen.*

Tuesday, Fourth Week of Lent

Falling Into Sin

At times falling is something that cannot be helped. We may be beaten down and exhausted as Jesus was or we might trip over something. Sometimes it may be easy to get right back up and carry on, and the only thing that might have been hurt could be our pride. Other times it is a major effort to pull ourselves up and continue on as Jesus did. Sometimes we cannot get up by ourselves. We hear stories of elderly people who have lain on the floor in their homes for hours because they have fallen and cannot get up.

We fall into sin. Sometimes it is a lesser sin, perhaps an unkind work spoken. We recognize that we have erred, offer an apology, seek forgiveness and move on. Prayer and our conscience may help us to keep from recommitting these acts, but we may find ourselves tempted and sin again.

At other times our sins are grievous ones; we have fallen into evil ways. We may be lying, cheating or stealing. We may be doing so to cover up fraud, gambling debts, or drug abuse. We may end up in prison if we have committed criminal acts.

We cannot always see or want to see the error of our ways. It may take a counselor, a priest, or God directly intervening, to help us get back on the straight and narrow path. It may be very difficult, especially if we have become addicted to our sin. We may slip back into old patterns of sin again and again. The temptation is too much and we succumb.

Falling into sin happens. Just as Jesus fell again and again, we fall again and again. We are tempted and we sin. Sometimes getting back on the right track is fairly easy; sometimes it is tremendously difficult to do so. What we have, just as Jesus had, is a loving Father. God's love helps us to rise up from our fallen state and return to a state of grace. And we have the Holy Spirit to guide us. We just have to ask.

Loving and forgiving God, we stand before you sinful, sorrowful and repentant. Forgive our sins. Restore us to a state of grace and send your Spirit to guide us on the path of righteousness and obedience to your will. In the name of Jesus Christ our Savior we pray. *Amen.*

Wednesday, Fourth Week of Lent

They Fell To The Ground And Were Overcome By Fear

"When the disciples heard this, they fell to the ground and were overcome by fear." (Matthew 17:6) Is this after Jesus is taken away by "police from the chief priests and the Pharisees" (John 18:3)? Are the disciples hiding out in fear of the Roman soldiers? Is this when "the doors of the house where the disciples had met were locked for fear of the Jews" (John 20:19)?

No, this was not a moment of fear of capture or imprisonment. No one was threatening the disciples. The meaning of the word "fear" is better interpreted in other sources as "awe." In this case it was the word of God that brought the disciples down.

At this point in the Gospel of Matthew, Jesus has led Peter, James and John up to the top of a mountain and he has been transformed before them. Then "suddenly a bright cloud overshadowed them, and from the cloud a voice said, 'This is my Son, the Beloved; with him I am well pleased; listen to him!'" (Matthew 17:5) This is the fear of those who have heard the word of God directly. Jesus responds to their very human reaction with an equally moving human gesture: "But Jesus came and touched them, saying, 'Get up and do not be afraid.'" (Matthew 17:7)

Fear, suffering, pain, and also awe, can drive us to our knees, or even knock us off our feet. It is difficult in such moments to just rise easily, brushing off our fear or awe. It takes time to summon up the courage to face whatever has downed us. It is always helpful to have someone offer encouragement and support, as Jesus did, in such times.

When Jesus fell while carrying his cross, there were no eager hands to help him up. There were no words of encouragement recorded in the gospels. How sad it was that Jesus had no one there for him as he had been there for the disciples.

Jesus, we thank you for your ever-present encouragement and support. Thank you for a helping hand when we are down and out. May we in turn reach out to others in distress or need, in fear or awe and lending a helping hand. *Amen.*

THE EIGHTH STATION

Jesus meets the women of Jerusalem

Daughters of Jerusalem, do not weep for me,
but weep for yourselves and for your children.

Luke 23:28

Thursday, Fourth Week of Lent

Jesus Meets The Women Of Jerusalem

"A great number of the people followed him, and among them were women who were beating their breasts and wailing for him. But Jesus turned to them and said, 'Daughters of Jerusalem, do not weep for me, but weep for yourselves and for your children.'" (Luke 23:27-28)

Indeed, Lord, we need to weep for ourselves and for our children. We are the sinners who called for you to be crucified, who led you to this path of pain and death. We are the ones responsible for the sorry state of our lives and of our world. We must move beyond pity for you and for ourselves and seize the moment to change our ways and the ways of the world.

These women of Jerusalem that followed you, Jesus, were the official mourners, the comforters, of that time. We, who call ourselves Christians, follow you, too, Lord, but you call us to a greater mission. We are called to cry out, not in sorrow and lamentation, but in urgency and with compassion. We must call out for renewed faith and hope and love.

Jesus, you call us to boldly proclaim our faith in God. You call us to offer hope and care for the sick, the suffering and the dying. You call us to practice faithfully your commandment to love one another as you have loved us.

Only when we truly follow you, Jesus, not just to Calvary, but to communion with our heavenly Father, will we find peace and joy. When our hearts are then filled with the love of God and the power of the Holy Spirit we can carry on your work in the world.

We can make this world a beautiful place, a safe place, and a healthy place for our children and our children's children. We can spread the good news of Jesus Christ throughout the world. God the Creator will look down upon his creation and see that it is good.

God, Give us the courage to spread forth your message of peace and hope, of forgiveness and redemption to all are brothers and sisters everywhere. *Amen.*

Friday, Fourth Week of Lent

Beyond Wails And Lamentations

In Jesus' time only a few wealthy women had any status at all, and usually their status was tied to their families or their spouses. Women were expected to keep their home and care for their children. A few women like those who followed Jesus performed charitable acts, but most stayed quietly in their homes, neither seen nor heard.

Jesus was surrounded by strong women like Mary, his mother, Mary Magdalene, and Martha. He recognized their leadership, their compassion and their support. These women were present at his death when most of Jesus' other followers had run away. They continued to provide leadership in the early church.

Women have always been at the forefront of missionary work, in their own countries and abroad. They nurse the sick and dying, they educate the children and they feed the hungry. Sometimes they work in areas of great danger and some pay the ultimate price as martyrs for their faith.

Today women have wider roles in faith communities and in the world. Some denominations allow women to serve as ministers, and in other leadership roles. The current Presiding Bishop of the Episcopal Church in the United States is a woman, Katherine Jefferts Schori. Angela Merkel is Chancellor of Germany and Hillary Clinton is currently the Secretary of State in the United States.

From the local level to the international stage women of

today are speaking out about crimes against themselves and their children. They are advocating for the right to work, for equal pay and for protection from abuse. Women are demanding better health care for themselves and for their children.

As a new wave of uprising against dictatorship and despotism sweeps through parts of the world today, women are seen as active participants. In place like Tunisia, Egypt and Libya women are part of the masses calling for change, demanding basic rights and better treatment. Women everywhere are working and praying for better lives for all.

Perhaps it is no wonder that the women were first at the Cradle and last at the Cross. They had never known a man like this man—there has never been such another. A prophet and teacher...who took their questions and arguments seriously.

Dorothy Leigh Sayers

Jesus, help us to continue to encourage and support women in all their ministries everywhere. *Amen.*

Saturday, Fourth Week of Lent

The Crowd

As Jesus was led to the place of his crucifixion, "A great number of the people followed him." (Luke 23:27) Who were these people? We have been told "the disciple whom he loved" was among them. (John 19:26) According to John, present at his crucifixion were Jesus' mother, and his mother's sister, Mary the wife of Clopas, and Mary Magdalene. (25) According to Matthew that group included Mary, the mother of James and Joseph, and the mother of the sons of Zebedee. (Matthew 27:56) Mark includes in this group "Mary the mother of James the younger and of Joses, and Salome." (Mark 15:40) These were people who loved Jesus and cared about what happened to him. Although they may not have been able to help Jesus these family members and friends wanted to be with him in his final hours.

We are also told of a group of women "who were beating their breasts and wailing for him." (Luke 23:27) The mission of these women was seen as a humanitarian one in those times, aiding those about to be executed. Jesus addressed them as "Daughters of Jerusalem." There was Simon of Cyrene and perhaps a woman named Veronica.

Who might be the others that followed along this sorrowful path? Were there other disciples, hanging back so as not to be recognized? Some men who were admirers of Jesus would aid with his burial: Joseph of Arimathea who provided Jesus' burial place and Nicodemus who helped Joseph prepare the body for burial. Perhaps they were in the group of people following Jesus also.

Some of the chief priests, scribes and elders were there; many who wanted to see Jesus dead. Were there others who had believed that Jesus was the Messiah and were grieving because they had been deluded? Probably there were the usual curious ones who were hoping for some kind of excitement. Maybe there were some folks just going about their business that got swept up in the throng along the route.

Some came because they loved Jesus; others because they hated him. Many more were probably apathetic. Little was known and remembered about them against the background of the ending of what has been called the "greatest story ever told." To anyone who might have been in Jerusalem that day, I would simply ask: "Were you there when they crucified my Lord?"

My dearest Jesus, those who loved you had to stand by helplessly and watch you die. Sometimes we are in that same position. We cannot always help those we love, but presence and prayer are always powerful ways we can support a person. Give us strength to stand by those we love just as your family and friends did for you in your hour of need. *Amen.*

Collect For The Fifth Sunday In Lent

O Almighty God, who can order the unruly wills and affections of sinful men: Grant unto thy people that they may love the thing which thou commandest, and desire that which thou dost promise; that so, among the sundry and manifold changes of the world, our hearts may surely there be fixed where true joys are to be found; through Jesus Christ our Lord, who liveth and reigneth with thee and the Holy Spirit, one God, now and for ever. Amen.

****

Love what God commands; desire what God promises. Sounds simple enough, that is, until what God commands conflicts with our own desires. Then we might think, maybe God will see it our way, if only we pray enough or plead enough or try to follow all the other rules. Or maybe this commandment does not mean that one "little act of sinfulness" is wrong; maybe it is talking about the BIG sins; not our little follies. To follow this line of thinking and reasoning is to place ourselves above the mind and heart of the God who created us and who knows us best.

It really is a good thing that God "can bring into order the unruly wills and affections of sinners." We do need the help of God to keep us focused on his ways and will for us. "We who are wearied by the changes and chances of this life," ("Compline Service," *Book of Common Prayer*, 133) can be so lost in that chaos that we cannot hear God's voice, cannot truly understand God's will for us.

81

We do want to know and to love and to serve the Lord. We want to come to understand that God's "ways give more life than the ways of the world, and that following [God] is better than chasing after selfish goals."("Prayer For Young Persons," *Book of Common Prayer*, 829) We do want to feel the true joy that God has for us, that joy that is found in God alone.

I have found a fullness of joy that is more than full. This joy fills the whole heart, mind and soul; it fills the entire person, yet there remains more joy that is beyond measuring.

St. Anselm of Canterbury

Abba, Father, you know what is best for us. Please give us your grace to love all that is right and holy. Help us to keep your commandments and be obedient to your will.

Grant us the gift of your Holy Spirit to guide is through the difficulties of our lives and to help us remain fixed on the righteous path that leads to the saving grace of Jesus Christ. Please bless our lives with the joy of knowing Christ and making him known to others. There is where our greatest joy lies. *Amen.*

THE NINTH STATION

Jesus falls a third time

For though they fall seven times,
they will rise again;

Proverbs 24:16

Monday, Fifth Week of Lent

Jesus Falls A Third Time

Although most versions of the Stations of the Cross mention Jesus falling three times, as many as seven falls are mentioned in some sources. The repetition of the falls—and Jesus rising again and again are clearly more important than the exact number. With each fall Jesus is weaker, closer to death. ("Way of the Cross," *Catholic Encyclopedia*, http://www.newadvent.org/cathen/15569a.htm)

Jesus has fallen again. He lies sprawled in the dust, the heavy crossbeam pinning him to the ground. Will he be able to get up? Can he will his body once more to rise from the dirt and move forward? How does he do it?

Jesus, you are now near the end of this last exhausting, painful journey. However, the process is not finished. You will get up again only to be laid down on and fixed to the cross. You will experience much more pain and suffering until your agonizing death. There is a final act to be played out here on Calvary.

Jesus, somehow you have to go on. You have to go on to complete the mission of the Father and you have to go on for yourself—and you have to go on for all of us. You will take these final steps, complete the journey out of love for us.

You came into this world on a mission, a mission of love, obedience and sacrifice. You have served faithfully, and you will to the end. Nothing less than full atonement will do, and you will accomplish it.

Jesus, you raise your head and struggle to your feet, crossbeam perilously balanced on your beaten back. You fix your eyes ahead to an unseen place and stagger forward. You will go forward until you take your last breath. "It is finished." (John 19:30) Mission accomplished.

Jesus, thank you for your sacrifice for us, for the many times you struggled on through so much pain. Please help us to have the courage to walk this sorrowful way with you so that we will come to understand the suffering our sins cause. *Amen.*

Tuesday, Fifth Week of Lent

Humbled

"Humbled" is a word that does not seem to even begin to describe the condition of Jesus at the time of his crucifixion. Casual on-lookers may very well have described him as a beaten, defeated man condemned to death. They would have called him a failed prophet whose followers had turned against him, who had all deserted him. On the surface all these things would have seemed to be true.

Jesus accepted all the humiliation, the great agony he suffered, the horrendous death as a part of the plan of salvation. All this was an act of obedience to the perfect will of the Father. That act required that Jesus give his life in exchange for ours. He offered himself up for the sins of the whole world.

We are humbled by Jesus on the cross. It is we who were beaten and defeated men. Humankind had broken all of God's commandments, had failed to do the will of the Father. Paradise was lost. No human could redeem us or regain for us our place as children of God. Jesus chose to come among us, to live as a human, and to die a horrible human death. He took our place.

He humbled himself and became obedient to the point of death—even death on a cross.
Philippians 2:8

Jesus' many acts of humility, his bearing of all of the pain and suffering for us, his unfailing love for us demands that, at the very least, we walk beside him on the road to Calvary and that we stand near him at the cross. Solidarity with Jesus means we must acknowledge our sins and wickedness and confess them. We must accept the cross as a symbol of our human failure and of Jesus' triumph over sin and death.

> *At the Name of Jesus*
> *every knee shall bow,*
> *every tongue confess him*
> *King of glory now;*
> *'tis the Father's pleasure*
> *we should call him Lord,*
> *who from the beginning*
> *was the mighty Word.*
>
> *Humbled for a season,*
> *to receive a Name*
> *from the lips of sinners,*
> *unto whom he came,*
> *faithfully he bore it*
> *spotless to the last,*
> *brought it back victorious,*
> *when from death he passed.*

Hymn #435, Caroline Maria Noel,
The Hymnal 1982

Oh most gracious Jesus, you have taught us much about humility through your actions; give us grace to follow your example in your most blessed name. *Amen.*

LENT 31

Wednesday, Fifth Week of Lent

By His Bruises We Are Healed

*He had no form or majesty that we should look at
him, nothing in his appearance that we should desire
him. He was despised and rejected by others.*

Isaiah 53:2-3

Jesus, you were beaten, bruised and bloodied. You certainly must not have looked majestic in any way. Who would desire someone who had been despised and rejected? Who would want to be associated with someone who had been condemned as a criminal?

*But he was wounded for our transgressions,
crushed for our iniquities*

vs. 5

Jesus, you were an innocent lamb, led to the slaughter. We should have been the ones beaten and bruised. We should have been the ones made to suffer for our sins.

*Upon him was the punishment that made us whole,
and by his bruises we are healed.*

vs. 5

Jesus, instead of punishing us as we deserved, you took our punishment upon yourself. By your selfless action you healed us of our sins. By your suffering and death we were restored to our place as children of God and inheritors of heaven. We bow before you, Lord and Savior, King of Heaven!

*Crown him with many crowns,
the Lamb upon his throne.*

89

Hark! How the heavenly anthem drowns
all music but its own.
Awake, my soul, and sing of him
who died for thee,
and hail him as thy matchless King
through all eternity.

Hymn #494, Matthew Bridges,
The Hymnal 1982

Jesus, we cannot sing enough praise and thanksgiving for your healing grace. We thank you for your great love for us. We worship your as Lord and God of all. *Amen.*

THE TENTH STATION

Jesus is stripped of his garments

And when they had crucified him,
they divided his clothes among themselves
by casting lots

Matthew 27:35

Thursday, Fifth Week of Lent

Jesus Is Stripped Of His Garments

Stripping the condemned was a natural part of the preparation for crucifixion; the dead would have no need for clothes. It was also meant to be degrading. Such degrading acts were intended to remind the Jews that the Romans were in control. To the Jewish people especially this would have been an act of terrible humiliation because of their great sensitivity to nudity. Jesus may not have been very physically conscious at this time, but the Jews who were present would have been deeply distressed by the disrobing of Jesus. (*An Illustrated Stations of the Cross: The devotion and its history*, 1982, Rev. Jim Nisbet, 47)

The Roman soldiers chose to take the process a step further by casting lots for Jesus' tunic. "This was to fulfill what the scripture says, 'They divided my clothes among themselves, and for my clothing they cast lots.'" (John 19:24) The scripture referenced is: "They part my garments among them, and cast lots upon my vesture." (The Old Testament scripture referred to is Psalm 22:18)

The body of Jesus "would have been beautiful, the strong body of a carpenter in the physical prime of his life." (Nisbet, 48) Jesus, even in your passion your body is beautiful to me. It is beautiful to me because your love for me shines clearly through all the blood and sweat, the stripes and bruises. Jesus you are beautiful to me.

Jesus, your maimed body was exposed before all those present just as all my sins are exposed to you. The Father allowed the exposure of your damaged body to remind me of my own imperfections. You love me in spite of my imperfections; you see the good in me through all the ugliness of my sins. You love me both because of and in spite of them.

"In the experience of St. Paul, it is only when a person discovers that God really loves him in all his unloveliness that he himself starts to become godlike. Paul's word for this gradual transformation of a sow's ear into a silk purse is sanctification." (*From Death to Life: Forty Questions for Lent*, 1991, Frederick Buechner, 3)

"For this is the will of God, your sanctification."

1 Thessalonians 4:3

Heavenly Father, our souls are laid bare to you just as Jesus' body was laid bare to the world. You see all our blemishes, all our sins, and somehow you love us still. Thank you for seeing the good in us. *Amen.*

Friday, Fifth Week of Lent

Cover My Nakedness

Lord God, each and every day of our lives and on our judgment day we are as naked before you. You know everything about our bodies and our souls. All thoughts and desires are known to you. Nothing is unknown to you.

> *O Lord, you have searched me and known me.*
> *You know when I sit down and when I rise up;*
> *you discern my thoughts from faraway.*
> *You search out my path and my lying down,*
> *and are acquainted with all my ways.*
> *Even before a word is on my tongue,*
> *O Lord, you know it completely.*
>
> Psalm 139:1-6

All our sins lay bare before you, Lord. "O God, you know my folly; the wrongs I have done are not hidden from you." (Psalm 69:5) There is nothing we can do or anything we can possess that can hide our sins from you. And there is nothing we can do or say to take our sins away.

> *Wash me thoroughly from my iniquity, and cleanse me from my sin.*
>
> Psalm 51:2

Jesus allowed himself to be laid bare before the eyes of the world, to face humiliation and death so that our sins could be washed away, our bodies and our souls cleansed and purified. We are forgiven, we are healed and we are free of sin. Our souls shine bright with the dazzling light of God's saving grace.

LENT 33

Purge me with hyssop, and I shall be clean;
wash me, and I shall be whiter than snow.

vs. 7

Loving Jesus, you have taken away our sins with your cross. Please cover our lives with your grace and blessings, and cloak our soul with your peace. *Amen.*

Saturday, Fifth Week of Lent

Sport

Jesus, the soldiers made a game out of crowning you king. Cruelly, they fashioned a crown out of thorns: "And the soldiers wove a crown of thorns and put it on his head, and they dressed him in a purple robe." (John 19:2) They spit upon you. They also rolled dice to decide who would get your robe. It is said that evidence of that game still exists: "The large stones bear the marks of the soldiers' games." (*An Illustrated Stations of the Cross: The devotion and its history*, 1982, Rev. Jim Nisbet, 20) Your life and your death were irrelevant for any reason other than mockery and entertainment to a bored Roman soldier.

This cruel treatment reminds me of the bullying that goes on today. Children (of all ages) pick on others, treating them as inferior. The weapons of choice have escalated from the shoves and shouts and sticks and stones of my youth; today emails and videos are sent and shared that mock and humiliate classmates and neighborhood children. And, as always seems the case, special attention is focused on those that are perceived as different.

Lord, you had already been dealt severe punishment and were facing a death sentence. The soldiers were just adding sport to their orders. Today the humiliation and shame of bullying has sometimes led the victims to take their own lives. And too often bullies (and sometimes other participants) act out their need to control and dominate others with physical violence. The results have sometimes been horrifying scenes of the wounding and killing of innocent victims.

Those individuals who mock and bully others are often said to be disturbed people who feel inferior themselves and are cruel to others to cover their own insecurities. The feelings of power and control only escalate with repeated victimization. If only they could find some other path to walk, a path where they felt loved and appreciated, and didn't need to hurt others.

Jesus, your path to your death was just such a way. You did not taunt or even rebuke those who persecuted you. We need to pray that those who feel the need to hurt others will somehow find that your ways are the ways of love and life. *Amen.*

Palm Sunday

Collect For The Sunday Of The Passion

Almighty and everlasting God, who, of thy tender love towards mankind, has sent thy Son, our Savior Jesus Christ, to take upon him our flesh, and to suffer death upon the cross, that all mankind should follow the example of his great humility. Mercifully grant that we may both follow the example of his patience, and also be partakers of his resurrection; through the same Jesus Christ our Lord, who liveth and reigneth with thee and the Holy Spirit, one God, for ever and ever. Amen.

****

What a glorious moment! As we pause before Holy Week to celebrate Jesus' triumphant entry in to Jerusalem it seems as those time has stood still. "The next day the great crowd that had come to the festival heard that Jesus was coming to Jerusalem. So they took branches of palm trees and went out to meet him, shouting, 'Hosanna! Blessed is the one who comes in the name of the Lord— the King of Israel!'" (John 12:12-13)

On this day he entered the holy city of Jerusalem in triumph, and was proclaimed as King of kings by those who spread their garments and branches of palm along his way. Let these branches be for us signs of his victory, and grant that we who bear them in his name may ever hail him as our King, and follow him in the way that leads to eternal life.

from the Palm Sunday liturgy,
Book of Common Prayer

Here at last are people celebrating the coming of the kingdom of God on earth. It seems as though a veil has been lifted, that Jesus has been understood at last and we celebrate with them:

Blessed is he who comes in the name of the Lord.
Hosanna in the highest.

Imagine what it must have been like to be there. "Look, I see him!" "There is Jesus!" "God's kingdom is at hand!" Many people were spreading palm branches, others throwing their cloaks into the road. "Blessed is the Son of David!" "Praise be to God!" "Alleluia!"

God's people excited to see God's Son, the Messiah, has come at last. But, wait, do you wonder if any of those same people were in the crowds that shouted, "Crucify Him! Crucify him!"?

Jesus, We pray that some day we all will shout out "Hosanna to our King," and lay palm branches in your path as you approach the New Jerusalem. *Amen.*

THE ELEVENTH STATION

Jesus is nailed to the cross

By his wounds you have been healed.

1 Peter 2:24

Monday of Holy Week

Jesus Is Nailed To The Cross

Echoes of the pounding reverberate through the hills overlooking Jerusalem. Harsh metal rips through skin, tearing flesh. Stabbing pain racks Jesus' hands and feet and the sun beats down mercilessly upon him.

There is no justification for cruelty like this, or for murder. There was none then and there is none now. The human body and mind are creations of a loving God. Life is sacred.

Why did God allow such cruelty and why did he require the sacrifice of his life from his son? Perhaps it is to show the people of God just how cruel we can really be. We, who are created in the image of God, can do horrible things for money or power, in the name of justice, or even in the name of love. Maybe only the ultimate sacrifice could show us who we really are.

Mindless justifications were given for the actions of the temple leaders and the Roman officials. We do the same today. We find reasons to justify torture, assassinations and executions.

As Pontius Pilate and Lady Macbeth and others have found out, you cannot wipe the blood of human beings from your hands. God giveth and God taketh away. He sacrificed his son for our freedom from sin. How can we justify our actions? What do we sacrifice? Jesus said, "Father, forgive them; for they do not know what they are doing." (Luke 23:34)

Did those standing near the cross understand God's pain as well as his power at the instant of Jesus' death? "At that moment the curtain of the temple was torn in two, from top to bottom. The earth shook, and the rocks were split." (Matthew 27:51) Did God, on his heavenly throne weep as Jesus said, "Father, into your hands I commend my spirit."? (Luke 23:46)

Jesus, I weep that you must die for me. And I weep that my sins have led to your death. Forgive me, Lord. *Amen.*

Tuesday of Holy Week

King Of The Jews

When Jesus was crucified Pilate had this inscription written over his head: "The King of the Jews." The chief priests did not like Pilate having this inscription written on the cross of Jesus, so they went to Pilate and protested. Pilate's response: "What I have written I have written." (John 19:22)

These inscriptions were the charges brought against the criminal being crucified and were meant to be a deterrent. Apparently Pilate wanted to make an example of Jesus that many would see and clearly understand. "Many of the Jews read this inscription, because the place where Jesus was crucified was near the city; and it was written in Hebrew, in Latin, and in Greek." (John 19:20) Pilate did not want other rabble rousers stirring up treasonous behavior among the Jewish people.

During the questioning of Jesus by the high priest he was asked, "'Tell us if you are the Messiah, the Son of God.' Jesus said to him, 'You have said so.'" (Matthew 26:63-64) This was considered blasphemy by the leaders of the Jews as they did not accept him as the Messiah. It was Pilate who called Jesus "King of the Jews." When Pilate asked the Jews, "'Shall I crucify your King?' The chief priests answered, 'We have no king but the emperor.'" (John 19:15)

So what was Jesus? Was he "King of the Jews"? Yes, Jesus was king over the Jews, but his kingship was not some earthly throne but a heavenly one. Was Jesus the Messiah, the Son of God? We confess and believe this to be true, but the Jewish leadership did not. Out of fear of a kind of king or messiah they did not understand they had Jesus put to death.

> *In the Gospel, Jesus is "autobasileia," the kingdom himself.*

Origen of Alexandria

Jesus, you are not only the King of the Jews, but King and Lord of all creation. We bow and call you King and Lord of all. *Amen.*

Wednesday of Holy Week

Suffering

Jesus you know all of the suffering of human beings. You have lived it in life and you have lived it through your brothers and sisters. No one had words of comfort for you when you were dying. "And the people stood by, watching." (Luke 23:35) Instead you were mocked by the Roman soldiers: "The soldiers also mocked him, coming up and offering him sour wine, and saying, 'If you are the King of the Jews, save yourself!'" (Luke 23:36) And also by the leaders of Jews: "In the same way the chief priests also, along with the scribes and elders, were mocking him." (Matthew 27:41) Even one of the bandits crucified with you had no mercy. "One of the criminals who were hanged there kept deriding him and saying, 'Are you not the Messiah? Save yourself and us!'" (Luke 23:39) They felt no pity.

This sounds similar to what happens today. Someone is gunned down in a parking lot full of people, but not one saw or heard anything. A woman being raped and beaten screams out for help but no one calls the police. When gay children or adults are bullied or beaten others stand by and watch. Talk-show hosts claim it is God's justice when natural disasters take lives and destroy property.

Jesus, suffering did not end when you died on the cross, but you died for those who suffer. You spoke out against those who attacked or mocked the poor, the needy, and the helpless. We need to follow your example, but first we must acknowledge our own complacency and our complicity by our silence. Then we must work to replace hatred, cruelty and violence with the truth spoken in love, with justice, compassion and mercy.

The second thief rebuked the first one for his lack of compassion: "Do you not fear God, since you are under the same sentence of condemnation? And we indeed have been condemned justly, for we are getting what we deserve for our deeds, but this man has done nothing wrong." (Luke 23:40-41) And then he turned to the Lord of mercy and said, "'Jesus, remember me when you come into your kingdom.' He replied, 'Truly I tell you, today you will be with me in Paradise.'" (Luke 23:42-43)

Jesus, teach us your ways of compassion and mercy so that we can do to all our brothers and sister likewise. *Amen.*

Maundy Thursday

Here O My Lord I See Thee Face To Face

I kneel at the communion rail, having received the body and blood of my Lord.

Here would I feed upon the Bread of God,
here drink with thee the royal Wine of heaven;
here would I lay aside each earthly load,
here taste afresh the calm of sin forgiven.

All seems to fall away from me; I am no longer in church but kneeling before Jesus.

Here, O my Lord, I see thee face to face;
here would I touch and handle things unseen;
here grasp with firmer hand eternal grace,
and all my weariness upon thee lean.

Is this how the disciples felt at that first Eucharist?

Mine is the sin, but thine the righteousness:
mine is the guilt, but thine the cleansing Blood
here is my robe, my refuge, and my peace;
thy Blood, thy righteousness, O Lord my God!

Is this what heaven is like?

Feast after feast thus comes and passes by;
yet, passing, points to the glad feast above,
giving sweet foretaste of the festal joy,
the Lamb's great marriage feast of bliss and love.

Would that this moment could last an eternity!

This is the hour of banquet and of song;
this is the heavenly table spread for me;
here let me feast, and feasting, still prolong
the brief, bright hour of fellowship with thee.

Hymns #317, 318, Horatius Bonar, 1855,
The Hymnal 1982

O, my Lord and my God, precious Jesus, Thank you for the gift of your body and blood. As I receive you within my heart may I always recall your sacrifice of love. *Amen.*

THE TWELFTH STATION

Jesus dies on the cross

Father, into your hands I commend my spirit

Luke 23:46

Good Friday

Jesus Dies On The Cross

Jesus is dead. How can it be possible to hear these words and not be moved? Even if you do not know the gruesome details of death from crucifixion the images are stark enough to move you to tears. How could they have been so cruel? How could we have been so cruel?

The crucifixion of Jesus is about what happened then, and what is happening now and what will happen. Jesus was murdered by selfish, controlling people. Jesus was murdered by us. Jesus, I am so, so sorry. Please forgive me.

Jesus' death happens again every day when a child dies of starvation in this world of plenty. Jesus' death happens again when men, women and children are forced to live on the streets. Jesus' death happens again when the old and the sick go uncared for in this selfish world. Jesus' death happens again when the innocent are abused and violated. Jesus' death happens again when people are persecuted for what they believe or who they are. Father, forgive us.

Unless we find ways to feed all of God's people, children will continue to die of starvation. Unless we make an effort to provide shelter for everyone, people will be homeless. Unless we care for all the sick and suffering disease will continue to ravage and people will die alone. Unless we work to protect the innocent from predators, lives will continue to be devastated by abusers. Unless we learn to treat every person as a child of God there will be hatred and persecution. Lord have mercy upon us.

LENT 39

Jesus, many stood at the foot of your cross silent. We stand at the foot of your cross silent today. What will we do tomorrow? What must we do today?

Jesus, give us the courage to take up your cross and your place in the world. Let us lift your cross high as we challenge starvation and homelessness, neglect and abuse, persecution and hatred. Let us be your hands and feet, Lord, and speak your words of love and peace. *Amen.*

THE THIRTEENTH STATION

Jesus is placed in the arms of his mother

A sword will pierce your own soul too.

Luke 2:35

Good Friday

Jesus Is Placed In The Arms Of His Mother

How can any mother accept this? How could Mary bear it? The lifeless body of her son is placed in her arms. Should that sad day ever come for me I cannot imagine the agony of living through it.

Did you touch his beautiful, bloodied face one last time? Did you hold him tightly to you, not wanting to let him go? Did you whisper "I love you," or "goodbye, my son"? Did you cry out in anguish and grief?

Mary, from the day of Jesus' conception you knew that this was no ordinary child and that he would not lead an ordinary life. You accepted that gift and charge even though you had been warned of the pain it would cause. You loved and served your son and his Father well.

Mary, all of our love and devotion for you could never take away one measure of your grief, but maybe by loving your son with all our hearts and all our minds and with all our souls we can, in some small way, make his sacrifice and yours worthwhile.

Jesus, your mother Mary's love and devotion shames us into silence because of our sins. Somehow you found a way to forgive us even for the grief we caused her. May our devotions of your passion touch your mother's heart.

Jesus, bless us with the kind of love your mother showed for you and burn forever in our hearts your sacred love for us all. *Amen.*

117

Jesus, may her deep devotion
stir in me the same emotion,
Fount of love, Redeemer kind,
that my heart fresh ardor gaining,
and a purer love attaining,
may with thee acceptance find.

In the passion of my Maker,
be my sinful soul partaker,
may I bear with her my part;
of his passion bear the token,
in a spirit bowed and broken
bear his death within my heart.

Hymn #159, Latin, 13th c.,
The Hymnal 1982

THE FOURTEENTH STATION

Jesus is laid in the tomb

Taking down the body,
wrapped it in the linen cloth,
and laid it in a tomb.

Mark 15:46

Holy Saturday

Jesus Is Laid In The Tomb

Heavy weight they carried to that tomb with heavy, heavy hearts. Jesus, the Messiah, is dead. His body is laid in a rocky tomb. Is all hope gone now? Who to turn to for comfort and consolation? Who will be our savior now?

Jesus' disciples seemed at a loss. It is so easy to criticize. We were not there. We did not see his eyes close for the last time. We did not see the lifeless body. It is not so different when we face the death of a loved one. Many times we want to wake up from this bad dream, to see our loved one walk through the door. How long does it take to sink in that this is the new reality? We will never see that person on earth again. Who do we turn to now in our grief and sorrow?

But they understood nothing about all these things;
in fact, what he said was hidden from them, and they did
not grasp what was said.
Luke 18:34

According to the scriptures Jesus told his disciples more than once (three times in the Gospel of Matthew) exactly what was going to happen to him.

While Jesus was going up to Jerusalem, he took the
twelve disciples aside by themselves, and said to them
on the way, 'See, we are going up to Jerusalem, and the
Son of Man will be handed over to the chief priests and
scribes, and they will condemn him to death; then they
will hand him over to the Gentiles to be mocked and

flogged and crucified; __and on the third day he will be__
__raised.__'" (Matthew 20:17-19) (Emphasis added; see also
Matthew 16:21, 17:22; Luke 9:22, 13:32, 18:33)

Hear again these words of Jesus. Hear them on this day
when he was laid in the tomb, hear them when a loved one dies,
pray to hear them and believe them now and when you are on
your death bed. "And on the third day he will be raised." Amen,
Alleluia.

Dear Jesus, from the silence of your tomb, we hear your
words of hope. May our ears be always open to hear these words.
Amen.

RESURRECTION SUNDAY

He has been raised; he is not here.

Mark 16:6

He is Risen

The darkness of the night sky slowly yields to the lighter shades of approaching daylight. The many creatures of the night slip quietly into sleep. All is still as the whole earth seems to pause for a moment of silence in breathless anticipation of the approaching day.

Now the shadowed light of early dawn has begun to vanquish the morning mists from the caves hidden in the rocky hillside. Light shades of blue begin to color the eastern sky. Birds call out the first greetings to the morning, to the beginning of a glorious day. A gently stirring breeze echoes a refrain: "He is risen. He is risen."

Suddenly the sun's rays burst forth over the hills, shrouding the land with bright light. The whole creation, refreshed and renewed, celebrates the dawning of a new day. The sad, broken world has a savior, has a fresh start. It is not just the dawning of another day but the raising of the Son. All of God's creation celebrates.

As the sun rises, all the earth seems to come alive. From the earth new blossoms and sprouts are springing forth. Creatures of all kind are breaking forth in chatter as well as song. Animals pop their heads up, other scurry about; all seem eager to be a part of the glorious day. The hills and the valleys are bustling and bursting with activity.

Darkness and death have been conquered. See, the tomb is empty. The Son has risen. He is risen indeed. Alleluia! Alleluia!

He is risen, he is risen!
Tell it out with joyful voice:
he has burst his three days' prison;
let the whole wide earth rejoice:
Come, with high and holy hymning,
death is conquered, man is free,
Christ has won the victory.

Come, with high and holy hymning,
hail our Lord's triumphant day;
not one darksome cloud is dimming
yonder glorious morning ray,
breaking o'er the purple east,
symbol of our Easter feast.

Hymn #180, C. F. Alexander, 1846,
The Hymnal 1982.

About the author

Author Diane Zike has a Bachelor of Arts degree in English Literature from the City College of the City University of New York and holds a Master of Arts Degree in Ministry and Culture from Phillips Theological Seminary in Tulsa, Oklahoma. She received her initial training in pastoral care while assisting in the Tulsa Episcopal Chaplaincy program. Diane completed a unit of Clinical Pastoral Education at Hillcrest Medical Center in Tulsa.

Diane brings a variety of life experiences to the writing of meditations. She was the chaplain and director for Interfaith AIDS Ministries in Tulsa for ten years. Diane served on the Diocesan AIDS Commission of the Episcopal Diocese of Oklahoma. She also worked in hospice and served on a regional advisory board for the Oklahoma Department of Mental Health. Diane has led workshops on hospital visitation, AIDS and death and dying issues and has written brochures and other materials on these topics.

Diane is a member of St. Peter's Episcopal Church in Tulsa, Oklahoma, where she provides lay Eucharistic visitation and leads a Wednesday Compline Service. She is working on additional meditation books for the Advent and Lenten seasons.

Via Dolorosa, The Stations of the Cross: Lenten Meditations is Diane Zike's second published book of meditations. *Annunciation, Incarnation, Manifestation: Advent to Epiphany Meditations* her first book of meditations, and her book of poems and prayers, *Here I Am: Poems & Prayers* were published in 2011 by Foolscap and Quill.

Acknowledgements

My gratitude is extended to those who have shared the Via Dolorosa with me; those who have walked and prayed the Stations of the Cross with me over the years. It has so such meaning for me. Thank you to the members of my St. Peter's Episcopal Church, Tulsa, Oklahoma Lenten study class and all others with whom I shared the first versions of these meditations.

Made in the USA
Monee, IL
07 July 2026

56546297R00075